This book belongs to

_____

Copyright © 2025 Grow Grit Press LLC. All rights reserved. No part of this book may be reproduced in any form without permission in writing from the publisher. Please send bulk order requests to info@ninjalifehacks.tv

Paperback ISBN: 979-8-89614-139-6
Hardcover ISBN: 979-8-89614-141-9
eBook ISBN: 979-8-89614-140-2

Printed and bound in the USA.
NinjaLifeHacks.tv

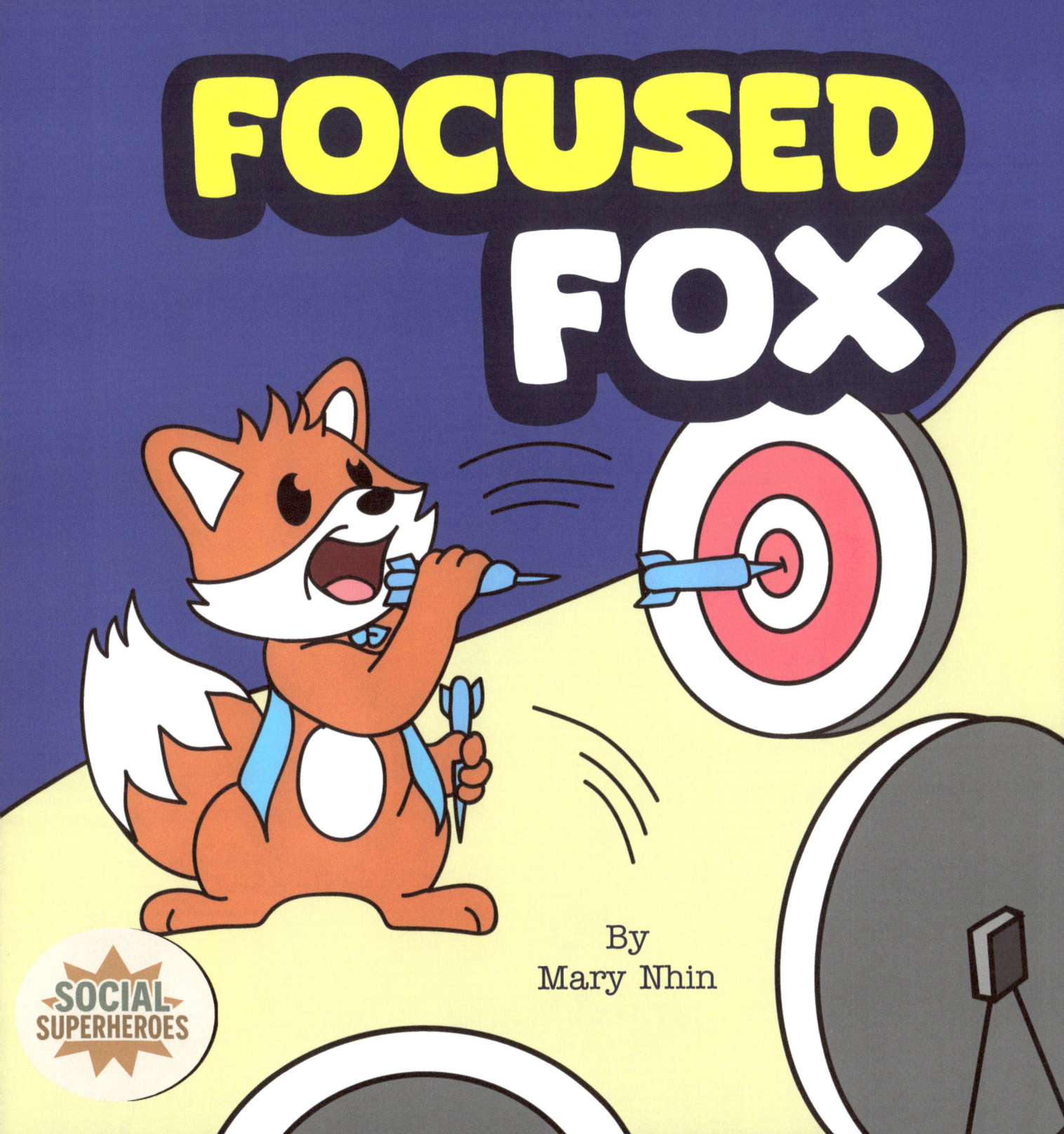

Focused Fox? Oh, *not quite yet!*
His mind would wander, his thoughts would jet.
When others talked, he'd hum a tune,
or daydream of flying to the moon!

In school, when Teacher Owl would speak,
Fox would doodle, tap, and sneak.
A look outside to watch the sky,
while lessons whizzed right on by!

During soccer, when the ball came fast,
Fox would miss—it *zoomed* right past!
He'd chase a butterfly instead,
while teammates yelled, "Where's your head?"

One day, Brave Bunny called him near,
and said, "Fox, listen close, you hear?
Your mind is quick, your heart is strong,
but focus helps us move along."

"Try my trick—it's called **F.O.C.U.S.**
Follow these steps—don't make a fuss!"
Fox perked his ears and tried to see,
Could this help someone *like me*?

F   O   C

"First, **find** distractions and get rid of them.
Focus your mind, don't let them win."
Fox looked up—his book was there,
but so was a bouncing ball in the air.

"Next step, **organize** your space,
a tidy desk keeps thoughts in place!"
Fox cleaned his books, his pencils too,
and guess what? His mind felt new!

"**Choose** greens to fuel your brain,
carrots, apples—not sugar or too much grain!"
Fox took a bite of something green.
Whoa! His focus was great and oh so clean!

"Move around! Shake, hop, or run!
Using exercise makes focus fun!"
Fox did a jump, a hop, a spin,
and felt his focus lock right in!

Now you're thinking!

"Last step, **split** big tasks in two,
one by one, you'll get things through!"
Fox broke his work into little stacks,
and soon, he finished—just like that!

Fox sat up straight, his mind felt clear,
no bouncing thoughts, no fuzz, no fear!
With **F.O.C.U.S.**, his brain felt bright,
and learning now just felt so *right*!

Next day at school, he took a seat.
He listened well, no tapping feet.
His paw shot up, he knew it all.
For once he didn't miss the call!

So if you find your thoughts astray,
Try **F.O.C.U.S.**—and you'll find your way!
Find distractions, organize things so it's neat and enough,
Choose healthy food, use exercise, and split up stuff!

Check out the Focused Fox Lesson Plans at www.ninjalifehacks.tv

 @marynhin   @officialninjalifehacks
#NinjaLifeHacks
 Mary Nhin   Ninja Life Hacks

 Ninja Life Hacks
 @officialninjalifehacks

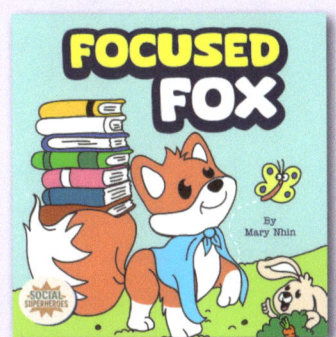   

 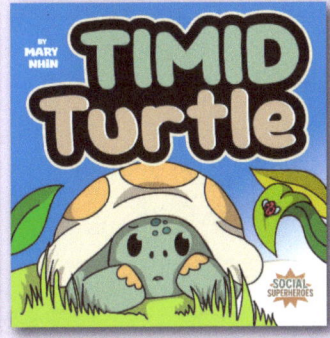 

www.ingramcontent.com/pod-product-compliance
Lightning Source LLC
LaVergne TN
LVHW070435070526
838199LV00015B/518

9798896141419